100 WORDS OF ENCOURAGEMENT

Unlock Your Greatness

By

Danario Lankford

CONTENTS

Introduction 3

30 Words Of Encouragement 5

Work Activity: Write the vision down and make it clear. . 9

18 Words Of Encouragement 10

Work Activity: Write what goals you will
achieve this year. 12

48 Words Of Encouragement 14

Work activity: Encourage Others 20

5 Words Of Encouragement 22

Author Notes 23

About Author 24

"I Will" AFFIRMATIONS 25

INTRODUCTION

Welcome to 100 Words of Encouragement: Encouragement is about giving support, confidence, and hope, but I love how encouraging words can uplift a person for the better.

Encouraging words can inspire people in tough times to not quit but to keep pressing forward in life.

I have come to realize just being more positive in life can improve a lot in life.

I say life is what you make it; if you give nothing you get nothing. Meaning if you do not put in the steps, the work and action on the things that you want to achieve in your life, then what do you expect to receive back?

The Choice Is Yours!!!

*Before you begin reading this book, please clear your mind and heart because this is your time to invest into you.

*Circle each encouraging word that has meaning to you.

30 WORDS OF ENCOURAGEMENT

---

1. A dream with action behind it can come true.

2. Everyday take advantage of your time because they print money not time.

3. You hold the key to unlock your own success so unlock it.

4. A clear plan with goals and determination is a wonderful way to achieve your success.

5. Recite your goals daily because they hold deep meaning.

6. Stop doubting yourself but believe in yourself.

7. Keep working at it, you will get there.

8. A man who takes care of his family is a great man.

9. Be true, be different, be unique, be you.

10. Ignite the fire that is within you and keep the torch lit.

11. You have greatness inside of you activate it.

12. Be optimistic, be innovative, be all you can be.

13. It is not a crime to dream so dream big and aim high in life.

14. Stop making excuses and make it happen.

15. Write the vision down and make it clear.

16. Complaining will not get you there, but action will take you where you need to go.

17. You are valuable, and you are somebody important so value yourself because your worth is priceless.

18. Always love and care for yourself, you matter too.

19. Great rewards come with kindness.

20. Fail your way to success meaning try go after it. You may not get it right the first or second time but do not ever quit keep going until you succeed.

21. Each one teaches one because iron does sharpen iron.

22. Always educate yourself and be willing to learn more.

23. You are created to live life abundantly so go thrive.

24. Praying is essential, it holds great power.

25. Be strong and very courageous in life.

26. Be a person that builds people up, not tear them down.

27. Do not despise small beginnings remember you have to start somewhere.

28. Mistakes are going to be made but learn from them and try not to make them again.

29. Go be blessed on purpose.

30. A positive mind is a healthy mind.

WORK ACTIVITY: WRITE THE VISION DOWN AND MAKE IT CLEAR.

What do you want in life?

_____

_____

_____

_____

_____

_____

_____

_____

_____

_____

18 WORDS OF ENCOURAGEMENT

---

31. Always look for the brighter things in life.

32. Faith has no limits so think big.

33. Do not let anything stop you from achieving.

34. Start creating positive habits to remove the negative habits.

35. Believe in yourself, believe that you can achieve it.

36. If you do not work you do not eat.

37. Never give up on yourself.

38. Build a belief system because every human being needs one.

39. I will win. I will succeed. I will accomplish remarkable things in my life.

40. You have the power to change the narrative for your life.

41. If you quit how will you see your wins?

42. Your time, talent and treasures hold immense value so cherish them.

43. You can rise above your circumstances; you are bigger than them.

44. Be the inspiration that the world needs today.

45. Small steps can equal a greater distance.

46. We all can learn to have patience in life.

47. Work at it and let the results speak for you.

48. If you want it, you will find a way to attain success.

WORK ACTIVITY: WRITE WHAT GOALS YOU WILL ACHIEVE THIS YEAR.

---

1. Goal:

Time Frame:

2. Goal:

Time Frame:

3. Goal:

Time Frame:

4. Goal:

Time Frame:

5. Goal:

Time Frame:

6. Goal:

Time Frame:

7. Goal:

Time Frame:

8. Goal:

Time Frame:

9. Goal:

Time Frame:

10. Goal:

Time Frame:

NOTES:

_____

_____

_____

_____

_____

48 WORDS OF ENCOURAGEMENT

---

49. A positive path is a rewarding path.

50. The reward is great when you do good and right by people.

51. When you are feeling a little down look up and smile.

52. Success and failure all boils down to decision making.

53. Self-discipline is meant to help you not hurt you.

54. Success is yours if you want it.

55. Be quick to listen and slow to speak.

56. Pain does not last forever, there must come sunshine.

57. Your past does not define your future.

58. Life comes with difficulties so stay strong and keep pushing.

59. If you want to go far in life, check your attitude because your attitude can determine your altitude.

60. When you affirm yourself every day it helps you to be more confident in your day-to-day life.

61. Yes you can become that person you always envisioned to become.

62. Starting your day off on a positive note is a wonderful way to start your day off.

63. The more you learn the more you can earn.

64. Life is what you make it, so make the best out of it.

65. Reading is a wonderful way to strengthen your mind.

66. Be willing to go the extra mile, meaning be willing to do more than others.

67. Stay focused and do not lose sight of doing good.

68. Poverty is just a mindset you can change it.

69. Become the change that you would like to see in the world today.

70. A growth mindset is something everyone should want.

NOTES:

_____

_____

_____

_____

_____

NOTES:

_____

_____

_____

_____

_____

71. When you compare yourself to others it can leave room for discontentment.

72. Change starts from within first.

73. Take it one day at a time, do not rush it.

74. You are created to shine, make your mark on this earth.

75. I have a spirit of love, power, and a sound mind.

76. When you find purpose in life there are no limits to what you can aim for.

77. Make your next move your best move.

78. Positivity always outlast the negative.

79. Replace fear with Big Faith.

80. One day it will make sense all that hard work and dedication you put in.

81. Doing nothing in life will not get you far in life.

82. Faith in action can make the dream happen.

83. You are phenomenal. You are a winner not a quitter.

84. Learn to welcome peace into your life because you deserve it.

85. Positive change is possible if you want it.

86. Note takers are money makers.

87. Trust the process, do not force it.

88. When you focus on the solution the problem is already being solved.

89. Take it one goal at a time.

90. The key to getting ahead is getting started.

91. All things are possible when you believe.

92. I am love. I am great, I am victorious.

93. Smile more often, it looks good on you.

94. Consistency is the key to success.

95. Do not ever stop believing, keep the hope alive.

NOTES:

_____

_____

_____

_____

_____

WORK ACTIVITY: ENCOURAGE OTHERS

Write down three or more people that you would like to encourage today. We all can use some encouragement.

1.

2.

3.

4.

5.

NOTES:

5 WORDS OF ENCOURAGEMENT

---

96. Your words hold great power so speak life to your situation.

97. Be fruitful, productive, and prosperous.

98. Ideas are powerful, do not let yours go to waste.

99. I am rooting for you, so make the best of it.

100. Today will not ever come again, so encourage someone today.

AUTHOR NOTES

You made it lets go lets get it. Clap it up and give yourself a pat on the back, you deserve it. I want to say thank you and I hope 100 Words Of Encouragement was of some type of inspiration and encouragement to you. This book was written to empower the reader to believe in themselves with full assurance, hope, confidence, love, and faith. Life is what you make it so go be great because greatness is upon you.

ABOUT AUTHOR

Danario Lanford was born and raised in Oakland California. He started his book writing career back in 2020 self-publishing his first self-help book ''Emptying Out the Negativity,'' Danario life mission is to reach people of all social classes to inspire readers to believe in themselves and to live a life of purpose.

"I WILL" AFFIRMATIONS

- I will love myself.
- I will be a blessing to others.
- I will aim toward greatness.
- I will keep pressing forward.
- I will win.
- I will succeed.
- I will keep believing.
- I will accomplish massive things in life.
- I will keep my head raised high.
- I will be the best that I can be.

Just know that you are more than enough. You are somebody so always affirm and believe in yourself. Always love yourself and do not ever give up on yourself because purpose is attached to the greatness inside of you.

Contact Information

Email: danario.lank@gmail.com

All rights reserved. No part of this book may be reproduced, stored in a retrieval system, or transmitted in any form without written permission from the author, except by reviewers who may quote brief excerpts in connection with a review. For information regarding please write to: Danario Lankford

Email: danario.lank@gmail.com

Made in the USA
Middletown, DE
27 November 2024